POLICE PSYCHOLOGY

CONNOR WHITELEY

No part of this book may be reproduced in any form or by any electronic or mechanical means. Including information storage, and retrieval systems, without written permission from the author except for the use of brief quotations in a book review.

This book is NOT legal, professional, medical, financial or any type of official advice.

Any questions about the book, rights licensing, or to contact the author, please email connorwhiteley@connorwhiteley.net

Copyright © 2022 CONNOR WHITELEY

All rights reserved.

DEDICATION
Thank you to all my readers without you I couldn't do what I love.

INTRODUCTION

Police psychology.

This is definitely an area of forensic psychology you don't hear about. I hadn't even heard of this great topic before I started to research this book.

I'm really glad I did because police psychology goes into a lot of depth about how the police work, how they could be improved, how they interview and so much more.

This great, easy to understand book will cover a wide range of police psychology topics from police bias and police culture to interview techniques (and how bad their traditional methods are) to the much more interesting forensic hypnosis and lethal force.

If you want a really engaging psychology book, this is the book for you.

Who Is This Book For?

Perfect for university psychology students and psychology professionals alike, this book is ideal for anyone who wants to learn about police psychology and how the police behave from a passionate engaging author.

I love this topic and this really comes through in the book so you know this WON'T be a boring textbook. This is a book you want to read!

Who Am I?

I always love to know who writes the nonfiction books I read so I know the information is reliable and comes from a quality source.

So in case you're like me, I'm Connor Whiteley the author of over 60 major titles including more than 25 psychology titles. Including the bestselling books *Forensic Psychology* and *Criminal Profiling*.

As well as I'm the host of The Psychology World Podcast available on all major podcast apps and YouTube.

Finally, I'm a university psychology student from the University of Kent, England.

Now we know each other, let's dive into the amazing world of police psychology.

INTRODUCTION TO POLICE PSYCHOLOGY

Moving onto police psychology, we need to cover some of the basics first and we need to understand why's police psychology important.

Therefore, in the Criminal Justice System, the police are the most highly regarded component with them surpassing other people like judges, lawyers, crime scene techs and more. (Howitt, 1986)

But what makes this interesting is people still hold them in high regard but they don't understand what they do or people don't know a lot about police activity.

And this I always think is an interesting part of human behaviour because we can like something without necessarily understanding why we like it, or know too much about it.

Furthermore, this high regard towards police

officers doesn't change when you show people objective evidence. (Christensen, Schmit and Henderson, 1982)

For example, if you were to show the police in your local area compared to lawyers were the weakest link in the Criminal Justice System.

Additionally, the nature of policing has changed in recent years with the Police force becoming a service industry to the public. As well as issues like security, harm reduction and safety taking over as the focus of policing from law enforcement and crime control.

Yet none of this answers the question why people have such a high regard for police officers compared to other fractions in the criminal justice system. Like, lawyers and judges.

Especially, when you could they're all as important as each other and some might say lawyers have a tougher job than the police. Since they need to take what the police gives them (which can be bad sometimes) and then they need to convince a judge or jury the police have the right man or woman.

It's not my opinion, I'm just trying to think about what is it about the police that gets them the high, and not equal or lower regard than other professionals in the System.

Why Are Police Regarded Better Than Other Fractions Of The Criminal Justice System?

But thankfully we can answer this question now because Elliot, Thomas and Oglogy (2012) conducted in-depth interviews with over 100 victims of property and personal crime.

With their results showing the high regard towards officers wasn't down to their amazing crime solving abilities or effectiveness or their ability to catch the criminals.

Instead it was down to something far simpler and more basic as well as with the police being the more public facing component of the System, it's only the officers that can do these things.

Since the high regard came from the police officers showing willingness to do their best to solve the crime, relate to the victim as an individual and not just another case in a respectful and personal way. Also the officers related to the person independently from the crime itself.

Overall, the researchers suggested the public want to be treated fairly and respectful by the police and when the officers showed the crime was unacceptable and they used non-blaming attitudes toward the victim and prompt action. This all lead to higher satisfaction.

To wrap up this conclusion, police psychology is the study of the police and police behaviours in an easy to understand definition.

Then the rest of the book can be broken down into a few different sections with us first looking at police culture and the negatives of that. Following this we'll take a look but very interesting look at interviewing and police interrogations before we finish up the book by looking at some of the great smaller topics. For instance, lethal force and forensic hypnosis.

I'm really looking forward to this book!

PART ONE: POLICE CULTURE AND BIAS

ed
POLICE PSYCHOLOGY

POLICE CULTURE

Moving onto our first 'proper' topic of the book, we need to look at the idea of police culture because it has dramatic effects on the police and how they operate as you'll see in upcoming chapters.

However, to get us started, the idea of there being a personality or set of traits that makes a good police officer is dubious.

Because if this personality exists at all, this is most likely down to the requirements of police work rather than a set of already existing traits. (Ball, 1984)

Personally, I'm not even sure I know what these traits would be. Maybe some are hardworking, caring, relatable, good problem solving amongst others.

But if you're interested in this personality idea, you should read Personality Psychology and Individual Differences because it shows what personality traits actually are. As I think in this case personality traits are being used as a buzzword and not what they actually mean.

Moreover, Ainsworth (1995) suggested two days in police work are never the same. Because the officers will have new suspects, new cases, reports, evidence and more to file each day. Different crimes will be committed and so on.

Leading to the training of police officers are a compromise between what is practical in training and what would be ideal.

With the earlier generations of police officers only getting on the job training. Which let's face it, isn't ideal because these young officers could easily learn bad habits from senior officers.

As well as Ainsworth (1995) discussed that past training focused on available powers for police and encouraged route training of legislation.

Now there's a growing emphasis on extensive training. Hence police academies, at least in the USA.

Also training is increasingly concerned with how to deal with the wide variety of incidents the police may encounter.

This is a good idea I think because when something happens to an officer they need to know how to react. Be it a bank robbery, chasing a suspect, being assaulted, etc. Officers need to know how to react.

How Does Training Affect Officers?

One of the reasons why I do psychology and explore it as much as I can is because every so often you find a very strange fact or something that surprises you about behaviour. And I believe this is one such thing.

Since the process of becoming a police officer leads to changes without the officers knowing.

Which I smile at because I find it amazing how we can change as people and not know how we've changed. Sure, I know the same applies to me but I think it's a strange quirk of behaviour.

To test this, Garner (2005) conducted a study looking at pro-police position and attitudes with police trainees through training and a year later.

The results found drastic pro-police position and attitudes changes on the trainees. But the officers believed strongly they hadn't changed at all.

Again, I think this is great. We know they're changed but the person believes they haven't changed in the slightest.

Culture:

Diving into the Police Culture part of the chapter, part of the training officers receive is on the job training with senior officers. Which as I mentioned earlier can be regarded as practical training and some senior officers may use practices that are less than ideal. Leading trainees to learn bad habits.

I'm mentioning this because it's important to consider when thinking about the occupational subculture or police culture.

In addition, Skolnick (1996) was the first to suggest the culture of police officers influence the work of the police force and this culture is unique to the police.

For example, the workplace culture in a hospital is going to be different to one in a school.

Furthermore, the police culture refers to the characteristic patterns of thinking, beliefs, behaviour and interactions that police officers share.

Essentially these are normal, accepted and prescribed standards for police personnel.

But this doesn't mean they're fixed or unchanging patterns.

Linking this to the beginning of the chapter, officers may be picked because they have the qualities that a good officer has but they learn and become indoctrinated into the police culture by interacting with other officers.

And I'm not trying to make the police sound evil and like they're brainwashing their officers because all cultures do this.

On the societal level, this is known as enculturation and socialisation.

On the workplace level, this is how we learn the norms and what's accepted in our place of work. For example, the professionalism required in a major company.

On an individual level, this is how we learn about our family culture and what's accepted in the home, family and social groups.

Nonetheless, this can be problematic as it can be at odds with what officers are taught at police college so it can cause some problems for the officers as they adjust to the reality of police work.

This feeds strongly into the next few chapters.

Also, it's the exact same in clinical and forensic psychology because we're taught the best way to treat offenders and reduce reoffending is rehabilitation.

(And yes it does work and we need to invest more in it. Read Forensic Psychology for proof)

But when we get into the real world and we learn about politics and budgets, we learn how little rehabilitation is actually focused on. At least in forensic psychology.

So that does lead to some annoying readjustment and learning of what reality is like.

Overall, the police force as an organisation exists in two parallels. Because the structural aspect deals with what should happen and is formal. Whereas the cultural aspects deals with what actually goes on in the organisation.

We're spoken about police culture, but what's cop culture and how does sexuality affect police officers?

CANTEEN COP CULTURE AND SEXUALITY

In the last chapter we looked at police culture as a whole and I introduced you to the idea of the police force exists in two aspects. The formal structural aspect which is about how the police should do things and the police culture is generally a description of the cultural characteristics of the police.

Then the informal cultural aspect about how the police actually work. We need to explore this more.

However, there is also evidence of certain attitudes within the police. As a result, for clarity's sake this informal culture is termed as Canteen or Cop Culture and there are positives and negatives about this culture.

There are a number of effects this can have on the police and we'll explore them throughout the chapter. But the first effect of this culture is there may be clashes between management and rank and file officers.

As well as Wotton and Brown (2002) gave a great summary of canteen culture as involving and valuing the police officer's mission, **pessimism**, action, conservatism, cynicism, pragmatism, suspicious, solitary and racial prejudice.

In addition one review suggested police culture has several important elements which were the above and I'll explain what they mean now.

Action is important because the police have a strong orientation towards action. Be it to actively investigate crimes and engage with protests.

This is further supported by Reiner (2010) who found that police officers are practical and down to earth in their orientation to get stuff done. Which is brilliant considering police officers need to be proactive to solve cases and interview witnesses.

However, this orientation towards direct action sounds good but it is also concurrent with cynicism about members of the community, so the police officers effectively doubt members of the community in which they serve.

Furthermore, and this one's interesting, the officers have a lot of pessimism about the police work can actually improve society. Which I think's interesting because you can see a version of this on TV dramas when some officers say what's the point of police work, there'll always be more criminals.

Yet I think the victims the police help would say differently.

Additionally, solidarity is very important to police officers because they need to know their fellow officers will support them.

You'll see this later in the chapter and in other parts of the book but this idea of solidary is a bit half-hearted. Because it generally seems like your fellow officers will support you but you have to be a certain type of person.

Building upon the solitary point more, police officers tend to be more socially isolated from the more general community and instead they socialise with the police community.

Which is all well and good but there should still be some contact and mixing with the community so the officers know what the community is like. As well as this could help the officers not to be so cynical about the members of the community.

The Negatives of Cop Culture:

Even though this does lead on from the last section, it needs its own section too because this is where we can get into the darker side of Cop Culture.

Since people use stereotypes and social categorisation to help us understand the world. (Social Psychology) Therefore, police officers use this too by stereotyping and categorising some groups within society in an evaluative manner.

Leading to officers to become suspicious of members of the community about the dangers they face. For example, they can stereotype black people and young men of all races as more dangerous and criminal than other members of the community.

Another negative of Cop Culture is the police's manifested moral and police conservatism because I'll show you in a few paragraphs time, the police does not like change. Be it sexuality, technology or female. The police doesn't like change on the whole.

Back To The List:

Referring back to Wotton and Brown (2002), all of the combination of traits they list as is best seen as an ideal type and a synthesis of police values and perspectives into a unified analytical construct.

Which hopefully you've found useful as I've talked you through it in one way or another as well as you can think of those values as a foundation of the rest of this Police Culture part of the book.

Moreover, that list isn't fully complete as some researchers argue that Wotton and Brown (2002) should have got beyond racial discrimination in their values and added some more elements. Because the following have all been described as characteristics of police culture:

- Homophobia
- Sexism
- Heterosexism

Now I should explain more about this but sexuality will be a focus in the next chapter but heterosexism is a term I've never heard of before and I didn't find anything on Google. But papers and textbooks say it's the preference of heterosexuality. It's the same as homophobia but it focuses on heterosexuality being more ideal and preferred.

It's rubbish of course but some people hate homosexuals for one silly reason or another.

Resistance To Change:

To add to what I mentioned earlier, evidence seems to suggest many features of police culture are resistant to change. (Loftus, 2009) because things were expressed to Loftus that heavily implied police officers believed their work to be a moral mission or crime fighting is central to police work.

In other words, because police work is a mission

and crime fighting, the officers don't want to be tied down to rules. Therefore, cop culture essentially determines the rules of policing and this allows them to be effective at their jobs.

But why?

Why are the police officers racially prejudice, homophobic and sexist?

I know lots of officers that aren't like that, why are the police like it as a whole?

Dominant Group:

Within all cultures there are tiers, classes, subgroups and more, the police force is no exception so now we need to look at how much damage (very undiplomatic I know) the dominant group are doing.

In the police force, the dominant group set the standards and rules of policing and what is effective policing for their fellow officers.

Again all cultures do this. I'm not trying to villainise the police, I do support the police.

Therefore, gay and lesbian officers can be seen as subordinate to the dominant groups. Meaning they can't come out and they aren't able to challenge the homophobia in police culture.

All in all because they have no power in the

police force. Sure they can come out and express their homosexuality but the dominant group will not be happy. This feeds into lots of other topics in psychology. For example, Right-Wing Authoritarianism and Social Dominance Orientation. ([Personality Psychology and Individual Differences](#))

Then this dominant group sets the standards and rules for policing through social norms and policies and they create the cop culture.

Which has been held responsible for lots of policing problems. Like their lack of adoption of new innovations, how members of ethnic minorities are treated, lack of accountability and their zealousness to stick to conventional rules.

Also, Marenin (2016) argued many cases of the police using deadly force are influenced by police culture.

This is the tendency for the police to believe the dangers of their work are more important than objectivity.

Arguably this is another way of saying the end justifies the means and the officers don't have time to objectively assess whether a person is dangerous or not.

Instead they rely on the information and stereotypes that cop culture has taught them.

More on this in the Lethal Force chapter.

<u>The Cop Culture Process:</u>

From an officer's point of view, they become part of the cop culture in the following way.

After they join the police, the process of occupational socialisation occurs where the person's police identity might not be psychologically compatible with other aspects of their identity. Like their sexuality.

In addition, ingroup identification refers to the shared sense of common identity shared by members of the police force.

Resulting in the homophobic, heterosexists, and sexist parts of cop culture identifying gays and lesbians as outgroups.

Leading to an increased likelihood of discrimination and hostility towards gays and lesbians from the majority.

Of course, this isn't unique to homosexuals because women and ethnic minorities are not really tolerated within the police culture. Since they're different and 'other' from the accepted norms.

The main problem with these officers with their outgroup characteristics is their police identity and homosexuality (for instance) identities are hard to reconcile and handle.

Resulting in problems for them.

Let's explore more of the research on this topic.

MORE ON COP CULTURE AND SEXUALITY AND THE PROBLEM WITH COP CULTURE

Building on the last chapter, we know the theory and some of the research behind the negatives of Cop Culture but let's look at more of the research.

For example, Wotton and Brown (2000) studied officers that were deemed normal by police culture. As well as officers with 1 minority trait (like female) and officers with 2 minority traits. (such as female lesbian or black homosexual)

In other words, there were three groups in this study and perhaps it's easier to think of these groups as: the "normal" group, less "normal" and the really not "normal" group as deemed by Cop Culture.

Their results found after some complex statistical maps (that I'm not even going to attempt to explain in this book) that heterosexual officers were at the core and who shared similar experiences.

As well as lesbians and gays were not amongst this control. Instead they were clustered in their own group because of their shared experience.

Finally, the officers with two minority characteristics were periphery. Since they were separate from the majority heterosexual group and the minority groups.

What this means and shows is the majority and dominant group of the heterosexuals were, well, dominant and made up the majority of the police force.

Then this dominant group shunned the minority groups and made them outcasts for lack of a better term.

Nevertheless, what makes this really interesting is Wotton and Brown recommended that it was the heterosexual officers that come with their discriminatory attitudes that were the problem and NOT the victims.

Now this shouldn't be interesting or surprising but to put this delicately, it isn't abnormal for people to blame the victims of discrimination for this. I'm sure if you told some people about these findings there would be someone saying "Are you sure the gays weren't too gay and forcing themselves on the straight officers? If so are the officers really being discriminatory?"

That is an appalling way to think but that's an explicit way how the victims are blamed for when things happened to them. Be it gay or black people.

Therefore, for a major academic paper to recommend this explicitly, it's interesting and impressive. Especially, when you consider it was 2000 when at least in my opinion, this was very progressive language for the time.

Moving on, one reason why the social attitudes and beliefs of police officers are important is because of the considerable amount of discretion that officers have in how they carry out their duties.

Since they have a lot of power over civilians and the extent to which a regular citizen can openly challenge the police is somewhat limited unless you know about police rules and regulations. Which I don't and I doubt I'm the only one.

In fact the only rule or regulation I am aware of is in the UK (and probably elsewhere) a lone police officer can't arrest you.

An example of this discretion is when they make an arrest. It can give the officers a great sense of power, and as individuals and as an institution officers try to make sure this doesn't affect them.

Yet as we know from Social Psychology, good intentions only go so far and not totally effective, as the officer's attitudes and beliefs towards the suspect can potentially influence their decisions. This is explained in the next chapter on Police Biases.

Homophobia In The Police:

For example, indications about how homophobic the attitudes are of officers can impact policing can be found in Lyon et al (2005) who found homophobic attitudes are typical of US police officers.

In another study, officers were given a fictional crime scenario and had to judge if the suspect should be convicted. It was a morality scenario but the suspect was either a homosexual or heterosexual. Same scenario, different sexuality.

I hate to say it but the findings found overwhelmingly when the suspect was a homosexual, the police officers were much more likely to say the suspect should be convicted.

Normally in my books I try to give a bit of hope to minority groups after writing a lot about these areas. I have to admit I'm struggling but I will add that things tend to improve with time. In 1967, homosexuality was legalised in the UK and in 2014, England, Wales and Scotland legalised same-sex marriage with Northern Ireland doing it in 2020.

My point is it takes time but things can improve. If I was to rewrite this book in fifty years, I don't know. I'll probably be deleting homophobia is common amongst US police officers. It isn't as common in the UK public anymore so over time I think that will filter into the police force.

One can hope.

Beliefs On Criminality and Gender

Whilst we talk about police culture some more, there is some evidence that in police culture, officers have systemically different beliefs about the criminality of men and women.

As showed by Horn and Hollin (1997) who studied a group of police officers and a comparison group that weren't in the police.

Then by conducting a factor analysis after conducting interviews with the participants, the researchers found 3 dimensions underlying ideas about criminals.

The first dimension was called Deviance with these beliefs focusing on criminals are deviants that can't be helped. As officers tended to say "trying to rehabilitate offending is a waste of time and money"

Of course if you've read or done Forensic Psychology then you know this is rubbish because rehabilitation does work and it's a great way to reduce the chance of criminals reoffending.

I hate it when people say things like this!

Following this the second dimension was Normality and this was reflected in statements like "There are some offenders. I would trust with my life,". Showing some people believe criminals are or aren't normal people.

The final dimension was trust which was measured by statements like "I would never want one of my children dating an offender."

The way how this is linked to beliefs about gender is because there were two versions of the questionnaires. 1 had a female offender as the subject, the other had a male offender.

The results showed that participants believed women were fundamentally less bad (or deviant) than men and this was true irrespective of the sex of police officers.

As well as the police viewed offenders as less normal than the general public.

Although, they tended to see offending females as more normal than men. Just like the general public.

Overall, showing that there are clear differences in the beliefs of the officers compared to the general public and it's terrible or at least a little bad that the public and officers believe that criminals are deviant and shouldn't be put through rehabilitation. Since it works.

I talk more about this and show evidence for this in Forensic Psychology and it's such a great topic in case you wanted to check it out.

Problems With The Idea Of Cop Culture:

I'm sure some of you would have guessed this already or protested at some of the findings and points I've made about Cop Culture so now I'm going to explain some of the problems with the idea of Cop Culture. Because as psychology is a science we must always be critically thinking so we can advance as a field.

Therefore, it's obviously questionable if all police officers share the same core of police related attitudes. As well as Cop Culture can't be monolithic.

This is pretty clear in everyday life and I did comment on this implicitly in the last chapter because there are plenty of officers that aren't racist, sexist or homophobic.

As a result, researchers have shown there to be a number of types of officers which are to some extent differentiated in terms of their cop culture attitudes.

For instance, Cochram and Bromley (2003) identified 3 types of police officers. They found a traditionalist, cynics, and those who were receptive and accepted change types.

Also it's important to remember that rapid changes can actually occur within the police force as a result of pressure on police management from political sources, legal judgements and findings of reviews.

Yet I would like to add this doesn't necessarily mean these changes are taken on board. This is similar to quotas on board of directors because a board can give women more seats to avoid sexist allegations. But it doesn't mean the women and by extension these new changes have much power or equal opportunities. (Social Psychology)

On the whole, this does differ from country to country but they always mean the established practices are always under review.

Which if we return to my hopeful section above quickly, then this only adds to the hope. Because with everyone watching and monitoring the police, it means the sexism, homophobia and racist attitudes of Cop Culture can be challenged and changed. So everyone could become a police officer and help improve lives.

EXPLAINING POLICE BIAS

This is definitely a concerning topic because as I've mentioned in my other books and I talk about later in this book, the police have certain stereotypes and biases towards certain groups.

For example, as a young male, I'm always stopped in shops because it tends to be my age group that shoplifts. I am NO shoplifter but because I fit a certain profile, people's biases kick in.

Also these biases account for why black people are disproportionately stopped by the police when they're doing nothing wrong.

As a result police officers are at risk of developing negative stereotypes of different social groups because of who they interact with whilst doing police work.

Leading Smith and Alpert (2007) to propose that this can lead to a form of unconscious racial profiling leading to disproportionate actions against ethnic minorities during police work.

As well as I should add this isn't only about race. This also applies to socioeconomic backgrounds, ages and mere appearances in some cases.

Furthermore, Hispanic and black people have repeatedly been shown to be overrepresented in police activities. For instance in stop and searches.

As a result, Smith and Alpert (2007) argued that social psychology and its research into stereotypes can go a long way in explaining why this occurs. As well as please read Social Psychology for more information on attitudes and stereotypes.

Yet what's interesting is the authors claim racism isn't the root of this bias but the bias acts against black people.

Let me explain this because the authors aren't denying racism exists. What they're saying is the police officers do their work, interact with criminals and over time as they encounter more and more criminals. They start to see patterns leading to a false correlation and stereotype.

For instance, if a particular officer works a lot of shoplifting cases and the offenders all tend to be young white males. Then they will form a bias against young white males.

The same goes for black people because the police officers see a false correlation and develop a bias that acts against black people.

Now, the real terms for this is social conditioning and the illusory correlation bias. Which can make police officers believe black people are disproportionately more criminal than white people.

Therefore, an officer's unconscious racial stereotyping may be part of the explanation of bias according to Smith and Alpert.

In addition, a person's (including police officer's) attitudes, stereotypes and beliefs occur when the police have repeated contact with a certain social group, with stereotypes being the outcome of individual and social cognitive processes.

Illusory Correlation Bias:

This bias can explain or help to explain a lot of negative human behaviours because as the name suggests this is when some people see two events and make a connection when there isn't one.

For example, the 9/11 terror attacks were committed by Islamic extremists. Leading lots of people to see a connection with Islam and terrorism. Resulting in lots and lots of people believing Muslims are dangerous terrorists that want to kill people.

This is absolutely rubbish because not all Muslims are terrorists. In fact it's a microscopic minority.

To put this in a practical example along with other problems minority groups face, Hamilation and Gifford (1976) created two fictional groups with exactly the same behaviours. The difference was in the number of people in the groups because there were 26 people in the majority group, 13 in the minority group.

Their results showed people found the majority group desirable and the negative behaviours of the minority group were higher than there actually was.

Group Processes

We've already spoken about the individual processes with the illusory correlation bias. Now we need to talk about the processes happening at the group level.

Police officers are members of the community. As such they have the community stereotypes about certain groups of people and this becomes deemed as collective knowledge as well as beliefs about members of minority groups.

For instance if the officer is from a mainly white area that believes that black people are criminals and poor people that hate all white people. Then the officer is likely to believe this because it's collective knowledge and they haven't had any contact with black people to prove otherwise. Sure there are other ways to learn about black people and social groups you don't mix with but as I talk about in Social Psychology, contact is useless unless the people actually want to mix with outgroups.

Anyway, officers also have regular contact with criminals. Resulting in them developing schemas (deeply rooted mental representations that affect how we encode, store and retrieve information. Cognitive Psychology) about black people and crime, with these schemas activating to help officers in new situations based on familiar features of crime.

Consequently, because the officer's beliefs about black people as a group, this results in the crime being generalised from an individual act to a group act. Regardless of the individual minority group members.

In other words, if one loud-mouthed and rude black person committed a crime. Then their crime and attitudes get applied to the group. Leading the officer to believe all black people are loud-mouthed and rude, regardless of how many kind, amazing black people there are.

Consequences:

Why is this important?

Why don't we just accept stereotyping is a part of life and people need to learn to deal with it?

(I still can't believe I heard that once.)

The reason why we need to focus on this and solve the stereotyping problem is because the consequences can be very serious.

Due to African Americans are four times more likely to be killed than white people in encounters with police in the USA.

So in some cases stereotyping can mean death.

Driver Biases:

As I mentioned earlier, police biases aren't always about race. Sometimes it's about age and gender and driver biases are a brilliant example of this next section.

Since driver characteristics can produce biases in the police. For example, women drivers are less likely to be sanctioned and punished. (Makowsky and Stratmann, 2009)

There is a minor problem with the differences between male and female driver punishment because there are differences between different police areas related to this bias. But the overall evidence is still clear. Women are less likely to be punished or sanctioned.

There are a few reasons for this, including officers make these decisions on whether to punish or sanction drivers based on the smallest amount of information.

Therefore, the officers are basically forced to stereotype to classify the motorist. Thus, they do look at the driver's race, gender, age and so on to try and understand what happened.

Another reason why this occurs is for some reason there's a form of 'chivalry' that might make male officers more protective of female officers and drivers. Hence they're less likely to sanction them to protect them.

PART TWO: POLICE INTERVIEWING

POLICE PSYCHOLOGY

CONFESSION CULTURE AND POLICE INTERVIEWING

Moving onto our next section of this book, the reason why we'll talk about police interviewing is because you'll see throughout this section that it's possibly the most important aspect of an investigation. Since without interviewing, the police can't solve crimes.

And the reason it's in a psychology book is because effective (keyword) police interviewing relies a lot on the psychology literature. As well as it's only because of psychology that police interviewing has improved to the extent it has.

Interviews:

This might come as a surprise to you as it did me but the police don't interview everyone taken into custody. As Rovert, Pearson and Gibb (1996) found only 30% of people taken in were interviewed in

London.

The reason for this is because many minor offences don't need an interview and if the offender has already confessed then the interview isn't always needed.

However, interviews are common for some offences, these tend to be the serious crimes.

Also police interviews are largely carried out by junior officers.

<u>Interview Tactics:</u>

This is a much larger topic that is explored in different sections of this chapter but despite some psychologists believing coercive techniques during police interviews can increase the likelihood of false confessions. Police officers regard interviews as critical stages in their investigations. Resulting in them making use of interview tactics to achieve a confession.

Unfortunately some of these tactics are dubious. Hence the focus on these tactics by researchers and this chapter.

But before we dive into some interesting studies, we need to understand that a police interview is different from a normal conversation. Because the police officer is the main controller of the content, structure and direction of the conversation.

With suspects discouraged from challenging an officer's authority, interrupting or initiating conversation at any point.

Which is very different from a normal conversation because if we were talking you could challenge me, interrupt me and change the direction of the conversation.

Changes In Interviewing:

You'll definitely see this as we go through this section but thankfully police interviewing (like everything) changes over time.

As a result of in the UK, concerns about miscarriages of justice has led to multiple legal changes towards interviewing. For example, the Police and Criminal Evidence Act (1984) changed the ideology of police interviewing to discourage practices that courts found unacceptable. (Sear and Williamson, 1999)

Leading to the changes when resulted in sustained differences between police interviewing in the UK and the USA. Due to in the UK there are multiple principles which underlie modern UK training in investigative interviewing.

For instance, the interview should be approached

with an open mind and the function of the interview is finding the truth and not justification for prosecution.

These I think are very important changes because it emphasises that just because the police has this person as a possible suspect, it doesn't mean this person is the offender. They're just a suspect. They could be guilty or innocent.

Some other changes include that the interviewing officers should behave fairly, and recognise the special needs of different groups. Due to these groups might be more vulnerable to making a false confession. Such as people with very low intelligence.

In addition, if a police officer ignores these outlines and accidentally gets a false or unreliable confessions then this can have massive consequences.

Unreliable Confessions:

Unreliable and false confessions have evidence consequences for the prosecution of a case. Sometimes a confession is deemed as inadmissible in court so the prosecution aren't allowed to use it.

In addition, there are a number of things that can make a confession unreliable. For instance, questioning that is hostile and/ or agnostic, a confession that following an incentive of bail (or any reward for that matter) and freedom from prosecution (also known as immunity). (Crown Prosecution Service, 2017)

Also lots of research shows the importance of confessions to police officers. Such as Cherryman, Bull and Vrij (2000) got police officers to listen to real-life audiotapes of differentiating levels of good and bad interviews (as judged by researchers). Then the officers rated these audiotapes on a wide range of factors.

According to the results, the following factors are characteristics of a good interview:

- Appropriate use of silence and pauses.
- All information is released at the beginning of the interview.
- Communication skills.
- Appropriate use of pressure.
- Conversation management.
- Empathy/ compassion.
- Development of and continued rapport with suspect.
- Information is released appropriately.
- Knowledge of the law.
- Openminded.
- Interview has structure.
- Purpose of interview is explained.
- Planning and preparation.
- Interview is kept relevant.

- Officer summarises appropriately.
- Officer responds to what interviewee says.

Characteristics of a bad interview:

- Closure
- Apparent use of tactics
- Closed questions
- Creation of apprehension
- Leading questions
- Overtalking
- Inappropriate interruption
- Undue use of pressure
- Long and/ or complex questions

Moreover, the officers tended to rate the interviews as good when a confession or admission was made. This primary focus on confessions as good and overall Confession Culture will be a theme here.

Yet not all police interviewing is skilled.

Thus, how do you determine what is skilled police interviewing?

To answer this question Griggiths and Maire (2006) made some suggestions on the important parts of an interview.

They proposed an interview should start with open questions to obtain preliminary accounts of what occurred, and closed questions are only used to clarify things at this stage.

Then the interviewer should use probing questions to gather more detail. This might involve challenges to suspect about inconsistencies as well as the suspect could be asked to confirm whether the police summary is correct. Closed questions are okay for this.

As well as what makes a skilled police officer at interviewing different from an unskilled one is a skilled officer would keep unproductive categories of questions to a minimum.

Like the following types:

- inappropriate closed questions.
- Forced choice questions that might make them choose a certain answer.
- Leading questions that imply the preferred answer.
- Compound and complex questions are overly long and even contain more than 1 question.

In addition, in interviews, expressions of opinion are avoided as they can lead to responses from suspects and indicate the interviewer bias.

Interviewing Around The World:

Interviewing is different around the world because what the British police regard as deception and trickery could be regarded as a great technique in other countries.

Resulting in police training involves instructions on these techniques and part of the US approach is to present the suspect with a justification for their offence.

The reason why this is believed to work is because the officers are appealing to them psychologically regardless of whether or not the technique has any basis in law.

Then the self-respect of the offender is apparently redeemed by these excuses and this links to the offender's positive self-image. Since whenever any of us do something wrong we need to feel good about ourselves so we often tell ourselves lies to maintain our self-esteem and positive self-image.

(Like I talk about in the Shoplifting Chapters of my [Forensic psychology of Theft, Burglary and Property](#) Crime book)

Another strategy is to minimise the crime. For example to tell the offender that this was their first crime and they could have committed far worse crimes.

Again this is believed to work for the same reasons as above.

However, when it comes to interviewing there must be a line drawn between a police interview and a police interrogation. That's the focus of the next chapter.

Police Tactics In Interviews:

To wrap up this chapter, let's look deeper into the different tactics the police can use in their interview.

As a result, Pearse and Gudjonsson (1999) showed the police tactics used for far serious offenders (not used for crimes like theft and shoplifting) can be scientifically broken down into 6 categories.

- Robust challenge- these are direct challenges to the offender. Like suggesting the suspect is lying and this is often repeatedly used at several stages of the interview.
- Appeals- police officers might appeal to the suspect to tell the truth, suspect's good character and suggest it's in the suspect's best interest to confess.

This one's used a lot in police dramas.

- Intimidation- officers make the suspect understand the seriousness of the situation, and anxiety felt by the suspect are amplified to the max.

This category includes the use of long silences, use of more than one officer and attempts to manipulate the suspect's self-esteem.

- Questioning style- links back to what I mentioned earlier about the use of good and bad questioning types. For example, echoing the answer, leading questions and asking more than 1 question at a time.
- Manipulation- minimising the seriousness of the offence, minimising the suspect's responsibility, suggesting themes to explain events amongst other things.
- Soft challenge- soft, friendlier toned challenges to the offender that suggest they're lying and officers can try to reduce the shame of the criminal acts. This part can be used in child sexual abuse cases.

However, what I found amazing about these categories was the researchers found the greater the use of appeals, intimidation and manipulation tactics, the greater the chance the UK court would dismiss the evidence as inadmissible.

And I thought this was interesting because these are the tactics you see so often on TV, in films and books and I know it's entertainment. But as a watcher after a while you just sort of assume that the interviews and police interrogation are at least a little bit correct.

My question would be how many of those police interviews and interrogations on TV would actually be admissible in court?

POLICE INTERROGATIONS

After throwing a lot of information at you in the chapter before this, I wanted to break it up a little by looking at the topic of police interrogations.

There are two main reasons for this, the first is completely selfish because I use interrogations as vehicles for my fiction from time to time. As well as from a fiction standpoint interrogations are great fun!

The second reason is more professional because police interrogations are the popular type of interview that appears on TV programmes, media and books. Since it's dull to have a quiet, nice chat with the suspect so police interrogate the suspect to make things more interesting.

In truth the police interrogation does happen but it's mainly US-based, other countries tend to perform police interviews and not interrogations with suspects.

In addition, the literature on interrogations is

massive so it's difficult to get an overall impression of the methods used in interrogation. Since screaming and intimidation are only two methods that bring to mind instantly. There are others.

Although, there is an argument that many of the methods of interrogation focuses on individual techniques and not presenting a full picture of the underlying nature of interrogation methods.

In other words, some people argue the literature focuses too much on the individual experiences and doesn't provide an overall picture.

Which I can understand because it can be extremely useful to know the general behaviour trends of a given activity. But individual experiences are needed too, therefore a balance is always needed in the literature.

In an attempt to explore and give us an overall picture Kelly, Miller, Kleenman and Redlich (2013) reviewed the literature and after a lot of reducing and creating lists. They managed to create a taxonomy of six categories to describe interrogation methods. As well as an interrogation could use any of these categories.

Rapport:

Firstly, interrogations can use rapport and relationships as well as these work by their being mutual trust and a working relationship between the interrogator and the interviewee. Also, both of them understand the goals and needs of each other in the interview.

In addition, some methods in this category include finding common ground and experiences as well as expressing concern for the interviewee and the situation they're in. Making the interrogator appear kind and respectful.

This is definitely a category everyone's seen on TV, especially if it's US based, and I always feel a bit of empathy for the interviewee because we know the interviewee is trapped, and the interrogator is only acted concerned. Yet the problem is the interviewee has no power and are trapped. So I understand why these interrogator methods work.

Context Manipulation:

I'm sure this is just my fiction side kicking in but this is a lot more interesting and cruel. Since context manipulation involves the interrogation manipulating the physical and temporal environment.

With this being interesting because it includes methods like conducting the interview in a small or informal room, the interviewee being isolated before in the interrogation begins, choosing of the time of day when the interrogation takes place like night time.

Also night is important because the interviewee is likely to be tired and more vulnerable as well as psychological distress is certainly the aim of the game in this category.

(Probably why my fiction side likes it so much)

Emotional Provocation

This is another iconic category because the easiest way to explain this is the interrogator targets the interviewee's raw emotions with the hope that the suspect will provide more information.

Think of films and TV programmes where the interrogator talks to the suspect or captive about how they failed to save their family and how weak they were when their family needed them most.

Overall, these tactics encourage the interviewee to feel helpless (like the others), it appeals to their conscience and the interrogator carries out the interview whilst the interviewee is stressed.

Competition and Confrontation:

Stepping away from emotional manipulation, this category focuses on perception, since competition and confrontation is about making use of threats and perceptions of punishment to gain the compliance of the interviewee.

With the interrogator emphasising their expertise and authority over the interviewee. They also repeatedly ask the same question over and over as well as the interviewee is asked questions in rapid succession without a chance to answer.

Now we will look at this later but I need to stress here, this and the category above, don't have a role in policing, or good policing because as I'll explain later these tactics can make evidence inadmissible in court.

Collaboration:

I know this might sound similar to Rapport but the key difference here is Rapport has a degree of condensation and apathy to it. Here there's more consent because the interrogator and interviewee make a bargain, they both want to help each other in exchange for something.

So it's the complete opposite of the category above.

Moreover, in this category, the interrogator gives the interviewee lots of scenarios about how they can regain or achieve control as well as the interrogator offers incentives to the interviewee to give them the needed information.

In terms of policing, this category can be useful because it can be used to make gang members, accomplices and other types of criminals give up their friends in exchange for incentives. Like, immunity, reduced sentences and more.

Again in terms of entertainment, this can be an interesting one books and TV can play around with because the process normally involves getting the interviewee to betray their friends. Which can provide interesting entertainment for the viewers or readers, if done correctly of course.

Presentation of Evidence:

Now this one I do love because it's brilliant, craft, cunning, an excellent category that I think it's so wrong, but so right. Probably only because I love watching TV where this happens.

Anyway, presentation of evidence includes the interrogator showing the interviewee a range of evidence to make them see the interviewer is powerful and the case is ironclad against them or their friends. Hopefully making the interviewee reveal more information.

This can include providing the interviewee with photos, witnesses statements as well as using polygraphic or other physiological measures about the offender's involvement.

However, sometimes, this can take a "darker" turn when the interviewee is confronted with fabricated or partially fabricated evidence. Which can have advantages and disadvantages.

But even though the whole police interrogation concept is US-based, some of these tactics can be seen by British researchers who have been studying UK police officers.

THE COGNITIVE INTERVIEW

Most of the psychology literature shows the police and their interviewing practices use less than optimum methods, and we saw this in the last chapter.

In addition, the literature is filled with advice and plentiful amounts of information about the best interviewing techniques. Yet officers tend to ignore these recommendations from publications. Resulting in them using their far below perfect methods of interviewing.

Furthermore, Wright & Alison (2004) analysed a number of adult witness interviews in Canada. Their results found these standard police interviews can be characterized by:

- Frequent interruptions of witnesses by officers
- More closed than open questions

- Psychological techniques designed to facilitate victim memories were not used fully.

Building upon this, we've already looked at the common structure for an interview but it's possible that the officers doing the interview had a version of the events they were trying to pursue through the interview.

Therefore, with all these negatives of police interviewing in mind, it should come as no surprise that police interviewing techniques are often under intense and potentially dangerous public scrutiny.

Leading onto a much better way.

The Cognitive Interview:

The cognitive interview attempts to enhance the recall witnesses by using techniques from psychological research on memory recall. Memory recall is another term for remembering.

Also to oversimplify what I talk about in Cognitive Psychology, you need retrieval cues to, for lack of a better term, reactivate retrieval paths in the brain so you can remember events and information.

To the police this means they need to help facilitate and give the witness these retrieval cues to help them remember.

Therefore, since 1992 the cognitive interview has

been part of the standard training package used by officers in England and Wales.

With it taking just a few hours for a police officer to improve in their ability to, for example, obtain information from witnesses. (Memon, Holley, Mitone, Kohenken, and Bull, 1994)

However, the cognitive interview is not recommended for resistant to interview suspects or uncooperative ones.

In this case, it's recommended best practice to use conversational management approach. (Shepherd and Milne, 1999) Which Shepherd (2007) created a very detailed manual about how to conduct an investigative interview using the conversation management approach.

Basically, the cognitive interview relies on witnesses and suspects wanting to be interviewed and work with the police. This is the vast majority of interviews though.

Moreover, the cognitive interview involves building trust and confidence between the interviewer and the interviewee. This process is also known as GEMAC (Greeting, explanation, mutual activity and close).

Due to the initial greeting signals there's equality between the two of them, then the officer discusses the reasons for the interview and they discuss the agenda of their activities. As well as what routines are used in these interviews. Like taking notes and recording the interview.

Afterwards the mutual activities include monitoring activities. For example, active listening.

Lastly, the close gives the opportunity for the police officer to summarise what has been said to check if the details are accurate.

Cognitive Interview Principles:

The original cognitive interview uses basic principles. (Geiselman, Fisher, Firstenberg, Hutton, Sullivan, Avetisscan and Prosk, 1984)

For example, getting the witnesses to recall in an environment that reproduces features of the original encoding context is likely to be superior. (Tulving, 1974)

In other words, if the police were investigating a bank robbery then it could help to take the witness back to a bank to help recreate the environment.

Also, memory is a complex thing and no memory is stored as a complete memory in the brain. As well as different sections or parts of the memory are stored in different places. Therefore, different strategies are needed to tap into the entirely of a memory.

To solve this the cognitive interview consists of four strategies to improve the memory recall of eyewitnesses. As well as incorporating these simple strategies have been found to improve eyewitness memory compared to standard police interviews.

One of those strategies is getting the witness to report every detail and little thing of the witnessed event regardless of how trivial it seems.

Another strategy is getting the witness to mentally recreate the circumstances of the witnessing. Including their feelings at the time, the noises and what was happening at the place of the event.

Therefore, from the start of the interview it should be explained that the witness needs to try and recreate the external physical environment and their internal state. Including their affect, physiological ad cognitive states. (Fisher, Brennan and McCauley, 2002)

Thankfully the cognitive interview uses various retrieval methods and encourages the witness to recall events from different points using different cues.

Now I know this might sound silly and pointless but the idea is that research has shown different components of a complex event can be recalled when different cues are present to help memory retrieval.

Also, reporting the event from an alternative perspective. For example from the offender, other witnesses or from another physical location.

In addition, as the cognitive interview has become more popular, more considerations have been added. Like concentrate on senses because in memories are encoded in terms of concepts but sensory features too.

As a result, getting the witness to close their eyes and visualise the event is helpful.

Personally, I think the cognitive interview is a great tool and you'll see why in future chapters but the cognitive interview allows the police to get better, more reliable information from witnesses compared to their standard police interviews.

This is a critical topic within police psychology so please enjoy learning about it in the coming chapters.

Problems But Not Memory Related:

We'll explore this topic a bit more in the coming chapters but there are a number of problems with the cognitive interview. Yet thankfully these aren't memory related, because if they were memory related then the entire idea of the cognitive interview being reliable could turn to ash.

One of these problems is that the witness may be

nervous, anxious, inarticulate and very unsure about what is expected from them in the interview.

This is why it's important to stress what the officers want from the start but even that isn't likely to work.

So a solution was created.

Leading to Fisher and Geneliman (1992) introducing the enhanced cognitive interview.

THE ENHANCED COGNITIVE INTERVIEW

Building upon what we learnt in the last chapter, it turns out that there are ways to improve the cognitive interview.

That's where the very interesting and useful Enhanced Cognitive Interview comes in.

This Enhanced version can be seen as the cognitive interview from the last chapter combined with techniques from communication psychology to help alleviate communication problems in the interview.

Like interview effective factors to account people's limited ability to cope with information flow. As well as to give interviewers techniques to help people cope with questions as a barrage of questions could overload the witness cognitively. Meaning they're only able to search their memory at surface level and not the deep, more detailed levels that the police officers need.

Nonetheless, an interview is complex for the interviewer as well because the police officer needs to frame the questions, listen to the interviewee's answers and take notes at the same time.

Leading to Fisher et al (2002) to create the Enhanced cognitive interview which hands control of the interview to the witnesses. To make sure they know they have as much time as they need.

Instead of the police, for instance, saying when the witness as recalled as much as possible. This is for witnesses to decide.

Which if we recast our minds back to a few chapters ago, this is extremely different to traditional police interviews that make sure the officers are in complete control. And witnesses aren't meant to interrupt the officers in the slightest.

Additionally, this amongst other things have led to changes in training. For example, training on the Enhanced Cognitive Interview focuses on the process of building rapport or creating an easy dialogue between witnesses and police officers.

Also there's a focus on asking effective questions. For instance, questions asked in a way that facilitates an understanding and a clear reply. As well as how to use appropriate body language to reduce the feelings of intimidation experienced by the witness.

This is important to bear in mind because even though the Enhanced interview gives control over to the witness, there will always be a power difference in the witness' mind. Hence, why it's important to stress there's a minimal power difference and this is, for lack of a better term, a safe space.

A final change is how to use pauses effectively. Due to using pauses can be a good way to give witnesses time to think and reply instead of rushing from one question to the next.

Overall, the main principles of the cognitive interview, including the Enhanced version, seems to be based on well-researched strategies to enhance memory retrieval.

However, just knowing the basics isn't enough. I mean of course you couldn't read these two basic chapters on the cognitive interview and instantly know how to perform it.

As a result Fisher, Brennan and McCauley (2002) explained that the cognitive interview should be done in five sequential steps.

Introduction:

In this first step, the officer should develop rapport with the interviewee and this establishes the appropriate social and cognitive context the interview to happen in. As well as the officers should explain the need for as much as detail as possible in the interview to encourage the witness to freely offer up information without a direct question.

Open-Ended Narration:

Next the interviews reach the open-ended narration step where the officer needs to allows the witness to freely recall what they remember of the witnessed event. This allows the interviewer to plan what techniques to use from the cognitive interview.

Then the interviewer makes notes on the recollection too.

Probing:

Here the interviewer knows what main recollections (memories) or mental images to focus on so the interviewer can use target these with techniques from the cognitive interview. Allowing them to get as much detail as possible on these focus areas.

This all helps to maximise the information gathered.

Review:

After the officers has done the other steps and the witness doesn't believe they have any more information to give them. The officers take the witness through the evidence to check for inaccuracies in the notes and recordings they have.

At this stage more information can be added and recalled by the witness. For instance, if the officer mentions something then that might trigger a retrieval path for the witness and they might remember more.

If this happens then unsurprisingly, the officer adds this to their notes.

Close:

Probably the least exciting part of the interview but this tends to include the fulfilling of official requirements about the interview. Like signing forms.

Then the witness may be encouraged to get back in touch if they remember new things about the event.

The Research and Problems:

It's clear from research that the cognitive interview works better than the traditional ways. But it isn't clear how it meets its objectives and how well.

In other words, it isn't clear how well the

cognitive interview meets its objectives and the purpose of the interview. Since some researchers question what the cognitive interview can be compared with.

It's really a comparison question. Not a the research is problematic or flawed.

Due to normally, the cognitive interview is rightfully compared to traditional police interviews because this is what the cognitive one is trying to improve on.

However, with traditional police interviewing being typically extremely poor and have a lack of appropriate training.

Is it fair to compare these two together?

Personally, I'm not entirely sure because I can understand where these researchers are coming from and I think they are right. But at the end of the day, the cognitive interview is meant to be improving police interviewing and help witnesses recall more information. Which it does. That's what I think we should be focusing on.

With these criticisms in mind, researchers have chosen to describe structured interviews as a control when measuring the cognitive interview.

As we saw in the Confession Culture chapter,

these more structured interviews are on the better end of the traditional police interviews. So not great interviews compared to the cognitive one but better than most traditional interviews.

As a result of these structured interviews contain the same good characteristics as the cognitive interview but they lack the memory retrieval techniques. (Kohenken, Thurer and Zoberbier, 1994)

All in all the research stills show the cognitive interview is better even against these more structured interviews.

Adaptions:

It turns out there's more than one adaption of the standard cognitive interview because you had the Enhanced version. But there is another version.

The Self-Administered Interview.

This is a new development in the cognitive interview that can help the police when they can't interview witnesses immediately. Because they could be overstretched or have too many witnesses to interview.

It was developed by Gabbert, Hope and Fisher (2009) and it uses some procedures used from the cognitive interview.

Overall, the interview consists of a booklet with

cognitive interview based instructions and questions designed to facilitate memory recall.

Now of course this doesn't replace a police interview but it makes sure the information given to the police isn't affected by the delay.

Furthermore, Gabbert et al (2012) found witnesses who used the booklet were better at recall a week later than people who didn't use the booklet.

Personally, I think this booklet is absolutely brilliant because it's an amazing innovation that further aids the police and it helps to combat one of the most basic problems with memory. As it allows the witness to write down what they remember so the chances of their memories being *tainted* from post-event information, memory reconstruction and other biases I talk about in Cognitive Psychology are greatly reduced.

I love innovations like this!

But how is the cognitive interview used in the real world?

THE COGNITIVE INTERVIEW IN PRATICE

After looking at the theory and evidence for the amazing cognitive interview, we need to see if the reality of this type of interview lives up to the theory.

Because psychology can still fall short of the expectations and the theory in real life, like so many other things.

As a result, it turns out there is some evidence that the cognitive interview has been well received by police officers as a whole.

However, there have been problems with implementing the cognitive interview more widely. Hence the need for this chapter.

Due to Memon et al (1994) conducted a study and found that officers that were trained in the cognitive interview still used some faulty techniques of conventional police interviews. But still use lots of cognitive interview techniques.

This is initially problematic because as we explored in the last few chapters, the cognitive interview is a great tool but all of its components and techniques are important. So the finding of officers not using all the techniques and relying on the bad techniques of the traditional interview is alarming to say the least.

Furthermore, officers viewed key parts of the cognitive interview as less useful despite being critical parts of the processes. Like changing perspective, various recall order and concentration.

Like I said earlier, these parts are some of the most important and they really help the witness to remember critical details, so it's alarming that these important parts aren't being used.

This is further supported by Wright and Alison (2004) who found most techniques of the cognitive interview were never used.

As well as it is unheard of for witnesses to mentally reconstruct the physical and emotional context of the event, and no one recalls an event of another respective.

If you're heard read or done Cognitive Psychology, then you'll remember the importance of retrieval cues and context for the retrieval of memories and two massive cues can be physical and the emotional context. So again this is bad that these techniques aren't being used. (At least from a theoretical perspective)

On the other hand, there are other cognitive interview techniques that are used a lot more frequently. Such as verbal demonstrations of the officer was listening to what they said.

This is broadly reflected in other studies. Like Dando, Wilcock and Milne (2008).

Resistance:

Like everything from progress to equality and everything that psychology tries to do, there is always resistance from others. The cognitive interview is no different.

Therefore, I have to mention there is greater resistance to the cognitive interview in other parts of the world or within countries. Since Compo, Gregory and Fisher (2012) described how in 1999, the US Department of Justice put out guidelines on conducting interviews with witnesses, based on the cognitive interview.

As well as the US was behind other parts of the world at this point because these guidelines were already well-established in the UK and elsewhere by this time.

In addition, the guidelines were well publicized and they were given to every police station as well as a training manual was provided.

So police officers knew about the cognitive interview. I don't see how an officer could honestly say they hadn't seen anything about the cognitive interview or an adapted form.

Yet when Compo et al (2012) listened to 26 interview audiotapes from South Florida and coded them for signs of the cognitive interview. The findings were very damming of cognitive interview's influence.

Their basic findings broke down into 25% of the questions were open-ended which is far below what the cognitive interview recommends, as well as the interrupting of witnesses and using example questions were common.

Additionally, the rapport building and cognitive reinstatement (again critical in the cognitive interview) was rarely used.

Also just over 10% of the questions were open with a narrative type answer. This isn't good considering it's the open questions that allow witnesses to think and remember details the closed questions missed.

Lastly, about 60% of the questions were closed

and the positive techniques of the cognitive interview were rarely used. But the use of long pauses were some of the most common techniques.

Overall, it's hard to say if all these negatives were down to lack of knowledge about the cognitive interview but the lesson in this study is same as elsewhere.

It's very hard to get interviewers to use with any consistency the full range of cognitive interview techniques. (We'll see some possible reasons for this in the next chapter)

Also this isn't only a US problem.

Furthermore, before we move on, I wanted to tie this chapter back to Cop Culture and remember how I said the police weren't open to new innovations. This is another explanation for the lack of take up since the dominant group in the police force probably didn't want to change their precious interviewing techniques so they might have discouraged their officers from using this new and better technique.

Always remember in psychology there is never just one cause. There are always many.

Impact of The Cognitive Interview:

We've seen the negatives and lack of impact the cognitive interview has made, but what about the positive?

It turns out there are lots and lots of studies saying the impact of the cognitive interview on memory quality is very positive.

For instance a meta-analysis by Kohenken et al (1999) compared the cognitive interview with various forms of the standard interview from over 40 studies.

The meta-analysis found that compared to the standard interview, the cognitive interview produced more correct details. As well as the time delay between the event and the cognitive interview, how involved the witness was and the laboratory the research was conducted in. All contributed to poorer outcomes in the cognitive interview.

Although, the cognitive interview tended to increase the number of incorrect recollections made and false memories all increased.

But this isn't as bad as it sounds because you need to remember the entire point of the cognitive interview is to get the witness to recall information and you're actively getting witnesses to recall things. So of course, there will be increased false memories along with an increase in correct details.

In fact, it is the type of cognitive interview that matters because the enhanced cognitive interview is especially error prone.

To clarify this while an increase in errors isn't ideal. What's important is the increase in correct details and if you calculate the increase, the cognitive interview produces a 40% increase in correct details compared to the standard interview.

All in all, whilst there are challenges in using the cognitive interview in the real world and we'll explore this a bit more in the next chapter. We need to remember the cognitive interview is still far better than the traditional and conventional police interview and that's what's important.

Creating and giving the police a tool that works and makes their interviewing better.

Saying that, do psychologists know best?

DO PSYCHOLOGISTS KNOW BEST?

After looking at the cognitive interview as well as other types of police interviewing, I think we can agree the cognitive interview is great. But do psychologists really know best?

I think this is important to look at because sometimes psychologists can get caught up in themselves and their own brilliance and ignore the reality of the situations. Which we focused on in the last chapter.

If we look at the literature, it's a great shame that the literature on interviewing techniques tends to offer a one size fits all approach to interviewing. Which isn't good because you need to use different interviewing approaches in different situations as we've seen in previous chapters.

Furthermore, whilst the cognitive interview offers a great summary of strategies when interviewing witnesses, these strategies can't always be used in real life. Mainly due to time constraints.

This is what I mean about psychologists getting caught up in their own work. The cognitive interview is great, there's no doubt about it, and the people who created it did a great service to the police, but the reality is slightly different.

Knowing this, we can now start to understand why police officers only tend to use certain strategies at certain times. We can think of these officers as cherry picking the best strategy.

In practical terms this is good because at least the officers are using some techniques. Of course it would be great if they used more techniques but at least they aren't relying on the ineffective traditional police interviewing all the time.

Moreover, more research is starting to show different types of offenders, respond more sensitively to the 'negative' strategies.

For example, Holmberg and Christianson (2002) showed that sex offenders responded more sensitively to the negative aspects of police interviews compared to murderers.

For example, sex offenders may respond aggressively at the passionate but increasingly confrontational approached used by some officers.

Leading some researchers like Gudyonsson (2006) to argue that sex offenders should be interviewed with an empathetic and/or understanding approach.

And before some of you reel back in horror that "monstrous" sex offenders should be treated with any kind of empathy and dignity. I wanted to say at first I understand where you're coming from but the literature shows that sex offenders can be treated and returned to wider society without being a threat to others. There's an entire section of Forensic Psychology dedicated to Sex Offenders.

As a result, in an attempt to find support for this argument, Oxburgh and Ost (2011) did scan the literature. But whilst there are many reasons why empathy is expected to work on sex offenders. The literature is quite sparse in reality.

It might be an idea for you to research in the future perhaps.

Overall, more research is needed before we draw any conclusions on what approach works best for interviewing sex offenders.

However, the lack of literature didn't stop them from researching it because Oxburgh, Ost and Cherryman (2012) researched effectiveness of empathy.

Also what's interesting about their study is unlike pretty much every other study in interviewing research. They didn't use getting a confession as a successful outcome measure.

Personally, I think this is better because these studies tend to focus on the content of the interview and how best to interview certain offenders, so the goal isn't a confession, it's what said and the structure of the interview. Therefore, the confession as the outcome measure seems a little odd.

Instead the study knows the police interview is meant to find out what, who, where, when and how.

Resulting in Investigation Related Information being the outcome measurement for the study.

In addition, the researchers obtained sample transcripts from real life cases from child molesters in England. Then they looked at the amount of empathy and questions type and how it (influenced) impacted the amount of investigation related information gathered.

The interviewing officers were trained in a number of interviewing techniques. Including the cognitive interview.

Afterwards, the researchers analysed the transcript and their analysis of empathy involved the empathy cycle (Barrett- Leonard, 1981) as well as researchers examined the transcripts for "empathetic opportunities provided by offender.

This is something that may indicate the offender is feeling emotional in some way with the officer could response with a "continuer". Which is a phrase, sentence acknowledge, emotion and they possibly provides an offender the opportunity to talk more about their feelings.

The thinking was these continuers make the offender more likely to open up to the police officer and reveal more investigation Relevant Information.

The opposite to a continuer is a terminator that stops the offender from continuing their feelings and shuts the offender down.

<u>The Findings:</u>

The study raised questions about the police showing empathy beside the empathetic opportunities provided by the suspect.

There were none.

Meaning the police officers didn't try to get the sex offender to talk about their feelings, open up and reveal more Investigation Related Information.

Additionally, the empathetic opportunities were only present in about half of interviews. As well as two thirds of these interviews were conducted by female officers.

Overall, the findings were very clear because use of good questioning types along the lines of the cognitive interview was related to the amount of investigation related information produced.

But empathy itself didn't encourage the suspect to produce more investigation related information.

Contention:

I really enjoyed learning about this short section because it proves how good the cognitive interview is on the whole from a legal standpoint.

Since as I mentioned in my Criminal Profiling book, and criminal profiling is NOT psychology and it isn't as brilliant as everyone thinks because you can't admit it to court every often because it's bad and has next to none research support.

Anyway, unlike Criminal Profiling, interviews using the cognitive interview technique can be admitted to court and as far as the literature knows, use of the cognitive interview is rarely contentious in the court of law, even in the US.

And textbooks and I'm adding the "even in the US" point because from my research and understanding of the US, lawyers like to raise lots of things as points of contention.

Furthermore, Fisher et al (2002) asked experts in the field and they're only aware of 2 cases (One American and 1 British case) back in 1990s where cognitive interview was raised as a point of contention.

This is brilliant and amazing considering only two cases back in the 1990s were raised as contentious. Which is understandable because cognitive interviews were new back then, so it supports the idea of the cognitive interview being effective and trusted in by the legal systems of the world.

Do Psychologists Know Best?

I know the vast, vast majority of people reading this book will be psychology students and professionals so we're all going to be bias a little.

But I think generally speaking we do know best because we created the cognitive interview and whilst it isn't perfect. It is still vastly superior to the traditional police interview which let's face it, is fairly rubbish.

Also psychology is very good at researching and generally we don't say something or recommend it unless we're researched it and it has research support.

So yes I think we do know best in general about interviewing and gathering more case related information and how to help police officers.

Because that's our job as psychology students, professionals, etc., despite what people believe, psychology is there to help people and improve lives in as many ways as possible.

And interviewing is just another way we can help.

OTHER TYPES OF INTERVIEWS

To wrap up this interviewing section of the book before we move onto some really exciting topics, we need to quickly look at some extra types of police interviews.

Since Leeney and Muller- Johnson (2012) suggested that police investigations can be thought of as a series of interviews.

This is interesting because it sounds like it really oversimplifies the process. But if you take a step back, you could argue police investigations boil down to talking to suspects and people, making connections from that talking and it gives you an offender.

Therefore, the investigation starts when the victim calls the police call centre (999 or 911 or whatever the local equivalent) then the call handler essentially interview victims to judge priority. This call handler interview starts with open questions then a series of close.

Afterwards a patrol officer is sent and they interview the witness or witnesses.

Thirdly the investigating officer interview witness further.

Following this, after information is gathered, a suspect or suspects might be interviewed.

Resulting in a decision being made about whether to take it to court or not.

Overall, as this oversimplification of an interview shows, police interviewing is central and it's a critical skill.

Leading to Leeney and Mueller-Johnson to explore this further by analysing 40 typical phone calls to an English police call centre that handles 70,000 calls a year.

Their main findings show that a typical call handler talks most of the time at 44%. Which is a lot higher than expected for interviews later in the process. As well as this interview only uses very few open questions at 2% of total questions. With the purpose of 89% questions used to gather information related to the complaint to the police, and the majority of these are yes, no, style questions.

In addition, about 11% of the questions were

unproductive. For example, these questions were either leading, forced-choice or suggestive questions.

However, what's interesting about this call handler interview is the typical call handler failed to write down 22% of the information given to them on records.

In addition, 43% of handlers used a call script which led to no loss of information and the number of unproductive questions were reduced.

But errors did creep in because 5% of the details were changed by handlers and 3% of details were added by mistake.

This to be honest isn't horrific when you consider how quick some of these conversations are and the purpose of these interviews are to assess priority, not solve a crime.

How Should We Regard These Interviews?

When I first read this section I was thinking that these interviews weren't perfect, especially because we just learnt how awful traditional police interviewing is. But let's look at this in more depth.

So there's no evidence of any cognitive interview technique here. Meaning the information from these interviews could probably be improved drastically.

But me and other researchers don't think it's

needed because these call handler interviews are clearly fit for purpose.

Sure, they aren't always accurate and the inaccurate information can prove misleading later on. This isn't good, of course.

Nonetheless, the speed could be a lot more important than the accuracy in this type of interview.

Personally, my thoughts here are if you're being attacked by someone and you call the police, you'll be *happy* to answer a quick few questions but you wouldn't want to be using any cognitive technique. You'll want the police to come and protect you. I know that's an extreme example but the same applies for if your house is being robbed and you're asleep.

Finally, it isn't clear if the cognitive interview and its techniques would add anything useful here because its time-consuming nature could make it inappropriate.

PART THREE: EXTRA FORENSIC PSYCHOLOGY TOPICS

THE POLICE CAUTION

Now we're moving onto one of my favourite chapters in the book, personally I think this is extremely interesting for a few reasons. But the biggest reason is (like you perhaps) I thought the police caution was the warning officers gave you when you commit a minor crime. For example, the officers say "We won't charge you, but don't do it again,"

But I was wrong.

Instead the police caution is the warning police officers are meant to give people when they arrest them.

Still I think this is as clear as mud but if I say Miranda Rights then I think everyone all over the world knows what I'm talking about now.

Since as US TV programmes are a major cultural export by the USA, people all over the world know certain things about American Culture including their Miranda Rights. And before this chapter I had no idea what the proper name for these warnings were.

Hence my interest in discovering they were called the Police Caution.

Below I've included the standard US Miranda Rights:

"You have the right to remain silent. If you give up that right, anything you say can and will be used against you in a court of law. You have the right to have an attorney present during questioning. If you cannot afford a lawyer, one will be appointed to you free of charge. Do you understand these rights as I have read them to you?"

Here's the Standard Police Caution used in England and Wales (Scotland and Northern Ireland have their own in the United Kingdom)

"You do not have to say anything, but it may harm your defence if you do not mention when questioned something you later rely on in court. Anything you do say may be given in evidence,"

Purpose:

Overall, the entire point of the Police Caution is to inform people of their right to silence and right to a lawyer, at in the USA. In the UK, the lawyer bit is mentioned most of the time at the interviewing stage.

The point of the Right To Silence is the legal principle that you do not have to answer questions from police or court officials. It's perfectly okay to refuse to answer the questions.

It's a common principle in most legal systems around the world, but it can differ. For instance, in Northern Ireland, the Right To Silence isn't an absolute right.

However, the reason why there's a chapter on the Police Caution is because there are problems with it. Since it varies by different amounts from nation to nation over time but there's a problem with how well people understand the police caution.

Before we dive into the research behind it, I want to explain a bit more about why people don't understand it because I was talking about this with family and they didn't understand the confusion.

So let me unofficially explain the problem with the right to silence.

You've been arrested and read the England and Wales Police Caution and your focus is on survival and making sure you're okay. You probably think silence might be your best option, but what if it isn't? What if your mind is telling you to say something?

After all not everything will be taken down into evidence. Even if it is written down it might not be admitted to court. Surely, talking is okay? The officers might understand it more if you explain.

Then let's say you convince yourself to say something. What do you say? What might you need to rely on later in court?

And that's the problem, the Police Caution for both the US and England and Wales aren't extremely clear when you think about it.

The Research:

In addition, research going back decades suggests in general the public have a poor grasp of the police caution.

For example, Shepherd, Mortimer and Mobaseri (1995) did a survey of the modern British police caution and found relatively few people understand.

I'll show you the parts of the Police Caution then the percentage that understood it.

"You do not have to say anything"- 27%

"but it may harm your defence if you do not mention when questioned something you later rely on in court"- 14%

"Anything you do say may be given in evidence"-

34%

And again the problem with the first and last section is it's conditional. The person arrested has no idea if they should say something nor do they know if it will be given in evidence.

Overall, in general the public doesn't have a good understanding of the police caution regardless of the country. Yet there is a bit of hope.

Scottish Police Caution:

In Scotland, unlike England, Wales and The USA, they don't have a precise prescription position. Meaning the wording of their police caution isn't given to them and written down. The Officer should explain it still.

In other words, there's no standard wording in Scotland.

As well as under Scottish law information admissible in court must be under caution and obtained fairly.

Also the meaning of fairness depends on the circumstances of the situation.

In addition, Basic common law is that the suspect can say something but isn't compelled to. As well as whilst there isn't standard wording for the Scottish Police Caution, Cooke and Philip (2008) gave a typical wording on Page 8.

> "You are going to be asked questions about assaults. You are not bound to answer, but, if you do, your answer will be noted down and maybe used in evidence. Do you understand?"

Personally, (I do have a minor bias towards Scotland even though I'm not Scottish) I do prefer the caution because as we'll see in a moment, at first glance it does seem easier to understand.

Moreover, previous international research shows young offenders have a problem with the standard caution because of a number of factors.

In other words, people don't understand basic rights and the problem with not understanding the Police caution.

As a result, Cook and Philip (2008) did a comprehensive study of all the different types and situations the police caution is used in and generally the youth offender found the Scottish Police Caution a lot easier to understand.

Additionally, Hughes, Bain, Gilchrist and Boyle (2003) studied what way was best to deliver the police caution. They got a highly educated and poorly educated group and gave the police caution to them verbally, in writing or a combination of the two.

Their results showed all groups claimed to understand it but objectively only 5% of the verbal group fully understood it. Then only 25% for the verbal and text group and 40% for the written group.

Leading the researchers to conclude it's best to give the police caution in writing and verbally for ease.

Regardless of the research, we still have a massive problem because 40% is extremely low considering how important the caution is. Especially when you consider that understanding it could be the difference between making a mistake and going to prison, or not.

The Police Caution In Canada:

Now in Canada things get even more interesting because Eastwood and Snook (2010) found a standard police caution in Canada but the problem in Canada is the police don't have to advise their interviewees of their rights. Canadians and Non-Canadians alike are protected by the right to silence and the right to a lawyer under The Charter of Rights and Liberties but the police don't have to remind them of it.

Anyway, Eastwood and Snook (2010) showed similar results to what's we've already seen in this chapter. Since only 3% of people in the verbal group fully understood their rights to silence compared to 48% in the written group. As well as only 7% understood the right to legal counsel compared to 32% in the written group.

Furthermore, many people that are arrested have limited literacy skills so it's problematic to give them the police caution in a written form.

So I'm afraid there's no perfect way to increase people's understanding of the police caution. There's always public education and TV adverts but as I mentioned in [Forensic Psychology](.) that's expensive and governments do have limited budgets.

Overall, the bottom line is normal people of normal intelligence don't fully understand the police caution and considering how important that is in law, that's terrible.

We need to fix this, but it isn't clear how to do it yet.

Do you have any ideas?

FORENSIC HYPNOSIS

Well. This is definitely an important topic in police psychology because forensic hypnosis is used by the police from time to time, sometimes it's admissible in court so we need to understand how the public see hypnosis and the media, TV and other forms of entertainment like to use hypnosis.

But how effective is forensic hypnosis in reality?

Before we answer that we need to see what hypnosis is about because as Wagstaff (1997) found. A clear, consensual answer of what is hypnosis is not forthcoming. (Wagstaff, 1997)

I would completely understand (because I would say it) if you said hypnosis is an altered or different mental state with a person maintaining their normal behaviour.

At first glance that's a good definition and that's the one that every single member of the public and most non-hypnosis psychologists would say to. But it turns out that definition would be ignoring a lot of evidence.

Jurors and Hypnosis:

We need to see how jurors and the public see hypnosis and we'll return to this point later in the chapter.

Therefore, the evidence shows that the public see a person experiencing "autonomism" because hypnotic suggestions are believed to make offenders less countable for their actions. (Roberts and Wagstaff, 1996)

Since the public believe that the offender isn't in control because it's the hypnotic suggestion making them do it.

It isn't how it works in reality because you can't make someone do something that they wouldn't do normally. But it's interesting to see what people believe.

In addition, potential jurors with experience of hypnosis are less likely to believe it affects behaviour. (Wagstaff, Green and Somers, 1997) Due to these people have more knowledge about hypnosis.

Problems and Hypnosis In The Investigation of Crime

As I mentioned earlier, hypnosis seems to be regarded favourably by the media. (McConkey, Roche and Sheeham, 1989) But many psychologists that are experts in forensic psychology tend to have less than enthusiastic views about hypnosis compared to other techniques like the cognitive interview. (Wagstaff, 1996)

Also forensic hypnosis does have a somewhat chequered history in court with the use of forensic hypnosis only really being popular in the 1960s.

As a result of this, forensic hypnosis has attracted a lot of controversy and legal ambivalence about where and when hypnosis is appropriate in testimony.

To try and solve these problems, the Hurd Rules (or Orne rules named after the famous psychologist Martian Orne) were created and these can be used as procedural guidelines as well as safeguards.

In addition, according to Lynns et al (2002), they briefly include:

- Recording of information- the information from the session should be recorded in writing or another acceptable form.
- Qualified expert- the psychologist or psychiatrist conducting the session needs to be trained in hypnosis.
- Independence- the hypnotist should be independent of any of the major parties

involved in the case and shouldn't be regularly employed by any of the parties. Including the investigation and prosecution team.
- All contact between the hypnotist and the potential witness should be recorded.
- Pre-hypnosis information gathering- a full account of the events should be gathered from the witness before the hypnosis session. The hypnosis shouldn't influence the description because the hypnosis interview technique could add details in error to the description.
- No other people should be present during the hypnotic suggestion phrase.

Furthermore, like a few sections in this book, there have been large differences in the legal systems of the world and here's another. Since the American judiciary tends to accept not reject hypnotically obtained evidence.

Additionally, if we cast our mind back to the beginning of the chapter where we spoke about what is hypnosis and the lack of a clear answer. Wagstaff argues the reason why hypnosis is still a source of contention is because hypnotised people do or can do the same things as a non-hypnotised person. Like, handle snakes.

Meaning that hypnosis isn't a distinctive state of consciousness because if it was distinctive, then they would only be able to do things that non-hypnosis people couldn't.

Of course, any given behaviour can have many different determinants.

Also there's an extensive academic research base into hypnotically induced testimony looking at its effectiveness and more. But of course, the hypnotic practitioners have a different view to the research.

Yet as this is a psychology book and psychology is a science, our main focus will be on the academic research, of course.

Thus, the academic consensus tends to doubt the value of hypnosis when compared with other techniques to improve memory recall. (Kebbell and Wagstaff, 1998) As inaccurate recall can result from hypnosis, decreasing the overall accuracy rate.

Moreover, meta-analyses of lots of studies by Lynn et al (2002) found that whilst hypnosis increases the amount of things recalled, it increases the amount of false recollection too. This is much the same criticism as the Enhanced Cognitive Interview.

It appears to be because witnesses simply report more recollections. Both accurate and inaccurate. As well as when asked to remember a fixed number of recollections, both hypnotised and non-hypnotised people show the same level of accuracy.

Suggesting that hypnosis is no better than people without hypnosis when it comes to recalling details and memories.

Furthermore, the very way forensic hypnosis is conducted is a problem. Which is why in the US, there are guidelines provided on hypnosis for legal reasons.

Another problem is that the hypnotic interview provides many opportunities for suggestions to be implanted into the interviewee's mind.

With Scheflin (2012) describing his involvement in a case as an expert witness involving hypnosis. There were a lot of the violations of the guidelines and errors. With the paper implying the guilty verdict and the long prison sentence could have been a consequence of these errors.

Like a lot of you when I first read this I was horrified that this could and would happen and I think it's scary to think that you would be imprisoned for a crime you didn't commit because of some people breaking hypnotic guidelines.

Of course, the court decided this person was guilty but it just shows the importance that as forensic psychologists or future ones, we need to be careful and thorough in our work to make sure nothing we do can increase the likelihood of someone going to prison when they don't need to.

A final problem for this section is how memory works. Now I can't explain it all in this section, if you want to know more then please check out Cognitive Psychology, but memory isn't a film of perfectly captured memories.

Instead memory is malleable and it can be influenced and change and reconstructed. Memories are changed all the time and it isn't hard to influence them. Because they're already influenced all the time from post-event information, leading questions, reconstruction theory, recalling the memory and so on.

Memory is not reliable.

Therefore, I give all the research in Cognitive Psychology and when this research started to come to light. It's been suggested that this led to the demise of forensic hypnosis from the 70s and 80s to this point. (Winter, 2013)

Return To Jurors and Hypnosis:

Using this knowledge we can now apply it to jurors because they might have increased confidence in hypnotised witnesses. Due to part of this is down to legal concern and witness confidence is very important to convince a jury of value of testimony.

Of course, this is all despite the increase in false recollections.

Effectiveness of Hypnosis:

We know that hypnosis isn't as amazing as we thought at the beginning of the chapter but it has to be mentioned that we should still consider the hypnotic interview better than standard interviews as it provides more recollection. But this is not due to the "brilliance" of hypnosis but only down to the poor technique of standard police interviews.

In addition, there has been lots of research findings based on generalisation from lab studies and there are some advantages to the cognitive interview as it outperforms hypnosis. Because the hypnotic interview could have distorting effects on memory.

As well as Wagstaff (1996) argues without detail knowledge of each hypnotism case and other details. It's impossible to draw firm conclusions.

Moreover, Berry, Robinson and Bailey (1999) suggested that regardless of effectiveness hypnosis still has number of effects for practitioners. Including the number of lengthy sessions needed and the aftercare that could be needed if the memories involved are particularly distressing.

All in all the study above is only pointing out the long-windedness of the forensic hypnosis and the possible aftercare needed. If we remember a criticism from earlier from the time-consuming nature of the cognitive interview, I think it's fair to say compared to hypnosis, the cognitive interview is lightning speed.

Overall, the value of hypnosis isn't seen as great in interviewing but there are still interesting aspects that remain.

For example, Hari, Wagstaff and Cole (2000) studied 2 techniques to help facilitate the memory of witnesses. 1 technique was a hypnotic technique that involved not reaching a hypnotic state.

The other involved a technique that originated from the cognitive interview and the results showed there was considerable evidence this may work better than the hypnotic technique.

However, it is still fair to say that despite all the problems with hypnosis, these techniques are still probably better than no technique at all.

Conclusion:

If you're looking for an objective conclusion at the end of this chapter, I'm sorry to say you won't be getting one.

Personally, with all the problems of forensic hypnosis and its unreliability and the potential to influence the witness' memory in negative ways. I cannot see any major benefits of using hypnosis compared to the cognitive interview.

Sure, both hypnosis and the enhanced cognitive interview do increase false memories but at least with the cognitive interview you have a good sense that these memories aren't being influenced any more than the normal ways. (Post-event information and reconstruction theory to name two).

So to finish up this chapter, I would say if you're ever on a jury. First, I would say lucky you, I would love to be on a jury.

Secondly, I hope you now know the pros and cons of hypnosis and if one of the teams tries to say hypnosis is the be-all and end-all. At least we all know this team would be wrong and probably only interested in influencing the jury.

POLICE AS EYEWITNESSES: HOW ACCURATE ARE THEY?

When it comes to witnesses that is already a lot of research that puts their creditability into doubt as most of a witness' usefulness relies on their memory, and as we know memory isn't always reliable. Just read [Cognitive Psychology](#) for studies and proof.

However, what about the Police? Are the police more or less reliable than the general public?

That's the aim of this chapter.

In terms of common sense, it's natural to assume to the police should be accurate witnesses because these are highly trained officers and their job relies on their skills. Including their observational skills which is critical for being a witness.

Also it isn't important whether or not they are actually accurate. What does matter is where the people making legal decisions think the police are more accurate witnesses. These people are also known as jurors.

As well as according to Clifford (1976) the majority of the public believe police officers are more reliable than the general public.

There is evidence that the same is true for other legal professionals. Such as judges and lawyers.

Nonetheless, forensic and criminal psychologists argue differently, and as I mentioned earlier the basics of memory and how it works means everyone (police officers included) can form false memories and reconstruct what actually happened. ([Cognitive Psychology](#))

One study demonstrated this when police officers and others that were asked to identify crimes that on occurred in a video on a street and their results showed that the police officers appeared to be no better than the civilians. (Ainsworth, 1981)

Actually, there was a difference in that police officers were more suspicious that a crime was taking place when it wasn't.

On the other hand, there are always two sides of each argument. As supported by Clifford and Richards (1977) who found that when asked to describe a person who had stopped them and asked for directions. Police officers gave better descriptions than others.

Then again when these encounters were briefer, there were no differences in quality for the descriptions.

Personally I think that's more important because if you think about the real world most crimes happen quickly and encounters with suspects and criminals are brief. That's important to think about.

In addition, Christianson, Karlson and Persson (1998) conducted a very gory photo experiment with different groups. With them finding the police were more accurate in their descriptions. Especially, when compared against schoolteachers. Suggesting that police officers are better witnesses in this study.

Experience:

If we take a moment to think about common sense and experience, how do you think it applies to this chapter?

I think it's logical to assume the more experience an officer has the better a witness he or she would be. But is this true?

Leading, Lindholm, Christianson and Karlsson (1997) to wonder whether or not experience in police service brings knowledge of criminal events which facilitates the way how officers remember certain events.

In other words, this follows on from earlier research suggestions that having familiarity with a particular domain of memory tends to facilitate the recollection of memories from that particular domain.

In terms of policing this means if a police officer has familiarity with a particular type of crime or even crime scene then this can help them to remember information and details related to that crime.

To test this, the researchers conducted a study of Swedish police recruit students and serving police officers and got them to watch a video of a crime.

The results showed the serving police officers were better and identifying the "offender's" knife when shown pictures of different knives. As well as the police officers were better at identifying relevant information.

A possible reason for the improved performance is serving officers see violent events more often. Resulting in less emotional responses from them and this gives them the freedom to focus in on the details and not based their memories on stereotypes.

<u>Operational Witnesses:</u>

So far we've covered a few types of witnesses in my forensic psychology books, we've looked at eyewitnesses and expert witnesses. Now here's a new piece of terminology for you and that's operational witness.

(I wonder how many more types of witnesses are there?)

An operational witness is, for lack of a better term, a working witness that has an active role in the case. Therefore, you could call police officers, emergency services and military personnel operational witnesses.

Since of these people have in common stressful challenges of their job and more importantly this mental demand could possibly impair their recall ability.

That's why this type of witness is important because it's very possible this stress and mental health could affect their recall abilities. Thus, making them unreliable witnesses.

As a result, Hope et al (2016) carried out a study with operational witnesses and non-operational witnesses. The active (operational) witnesses were told to take part in a scenario with an armed offender. The unactive witness watched. Then the active witness' heart rate was measured.

The results showed there was no difference in the accuracy of the accounts between the two groups.

And as the active witnesses physiological responses showed stress patterns, this was proposed for the poor performance of the active witnesses.

Yet both groups still showed high recall accuracy for the two parts of the study.

Overall, this suggests that despite people believing their training and observation skills make them amazing witnesses. The reality shows that their stressful job can impair their recall ability back down to "normal" levels and make them as reliable as non-police witnesses.

Extremely Good Memory:

We can all probably see from our everyday life that some people, like our friends and family, have better memories than others.

But some have really, really good memories.

As well as somehow the London Metropolitan Police recognised this so they have a small number of specialist officers who have extremely good memories, with them being able to recognise suspects from CCTV images.

And just to show how few these officers are, Only 0.29% of police and civilians workers are part of the group of Super Recognisers. As well as 69% of CCTV identification are made by this group.

That's a tiny number when you consider about the tens of thousands who work for them.

These people are what's known as Super Recognisers. Which is a memory phenomenon well known to memory researchers

To test how good these Super Recognisers were David, Lander, Evans and Jansare (2016) compared a group of police super recognisers, police non-super recognisers and the general public who weren't super recognisers. Then the participant did lots of tests. Like, the Glasgow Face Matching Test and the Unfamiliar Face Memory Array Test.

The results showed that both police groups were better than the general public but the Super Recognisers weren't better than the police Non-Super Recognisers group.

Also these "did better" statements aren't absolute because the groups didn't do uniformly better either. For example, these groups might have been the best at one test but not very good in another.

Of course, it could be simply put down to the unreliability of the measures used because no measure is perfect. Or some police officers could have better pop culture knowledge for famous faces than other officers.

Personally I would be rubbish at pop culture

questions and famous faces… don't even ask me. So I do understand this critical point.

In addition, super recognizers did make mistakes on recognition from CCTV images from time to time. Which is natural and to be expected, no memory can be perfect 100% of the time.

Conclusion:

Are the police more or less reliable than the general public?

That was the question for this chapter and like everything in psychology, the answer is it depends.

Overall, I would say no because generally speaking the police didn't do greater the public in memory and recognition tasks. Then there were other tasks that the police did do better than the public at.

So it really does depend.

But none of this matters.

And I'll mention what I said at the beginning, it doesn't matter what the researchers or we say about the reliability of the police as officers. This will always be the case until the people making legal decisions start to believe the police with all their years of service and training are fallible and don't have perfect memories.

Because like I'll mention in the final chapter, police officers are human and for this chapter that means that they have faulty memories. Just like the rest of us.

LETHAL FORCE

When you saw this chapter in the book description, I can guess you had one of two reactions. The first one being "Oh wow, we're going to learn about Black Lives Matter and police shootings," or you thought "I'm skipping this chapter. I don't want to hear about Black Lives Matters and all that,"

Both of you are wrong.

This chapter doesn't focus on Black Lives Matter and it won't focus on the disproportionate amount of black Americans shot and killed by police each year.

Instead the chapter will focus on lethal force in general and the psychology behind it. As psychology focuses on all human behaviours and using lethal force is certainly a type of behaviour.

Anyway, in the USA in 2016 135 police officers were killed and the murder weapon were mostly guns. (Chan, 2016)

However, police officers are more likely to kill rather than be killed. (Blan, 1994) with the US police killing more than 1,000 civilians in 2015. (The Guardian, 2015)

But why is this?

Why do the police kill people?

To answer that question, we need to back track a little and ask about the killing of police officers. Since some people would say officers are only killed by deranged killers.

But they aren't.

According to Blau, killers of police officers aren't mad psychopaths but general criminals attempting to flee crime scenes.

This is very important because this creates a strong cue to danger when officers see a suspect trying to escape arrest. As well as the following may be particularly dangerous about a suspect:

- Suspects who have dangerous associates
- Suspects with a history of being dangerous
- Suspects who work or line in place were violent and dangerous events are likely to happen.

Additionally, suspects and police officers have a buffer zone or a better way to think about it is a personal space bubble. Which when breached greatly increases the chance of the suspect reacting violently. (Blau, 1994)

The same goes for police officers because when a (perceived) dangerous stimuli moves within 1.2 m and closer. This is very likely to produce a dangerous response in the police officers.

Leading to lethal force.

Of course on paper (or your ereader), it sounds silly that something as simple as someone who might not even be dangerous getting close to you is enough for lethal force. But we need to remember in that moment, the suspect nor the police officer knows if the other one is dangerous and a threat to them.

The Cost:

After an officer has been involved in a police shooting, the cost isn't simply personal. Due to around 80% of US police officers left the police department shortly after their shooting.

Which can be a shame because it could be the loss of a great officer that would benefit lots of people.

I talk about this in the last chapter but I bet if we dig into the literature enough, you'll probably find most of them leave due to a lack of support after the shooting. More on that later.

Nonetheless, it turns out the officers involved in shootings tend to show certain characteristics. (And no before you ask they aren't trigger happy and brutal cops)

As a result of McElvain and Kposodia (2008) showed that College (university) educated officers had a 40% less chance of being involved in a shooting. As well as lower ranking officers were more likely to be involved in a shooting compared to a higher ranking officer.

This is mainly because the higher ranking officers tend to be behind a desk.

Furthermore, female officers were only 1/3 as likely to be involved compared to males in shootings, and officers involved in a shooting in the past was 50% more likely to be involved in another.

Finally, older officers were substantially less likely to be involved in a shooting.

Although, very different patterns exist for different countries.

Especially for countries with low levels of community violence and police that aren't usually armed. For these countries the figures aren't always available.

For example, as Rappert (2002) explains these figures aren't available for the UK but he still wanted to study it anyway.

Also for our international audience (Non-UK) I wanted to attempt to explain that our police forces are broken down into areas and counties. As well as the closest we have to a national police force would be the National Crime Agency but that focuses on crime all over the UK.

In other words, it doesn't collect data from all the specific police forces that you would use in a study.

Anyway like I mentioned Rappert (2002) still wanted to conduct a study so he had to rely on a collective initiative from a particular police area.

His results showed that the UK police force used lethal force in 6% of arrests compared to 20% of arrests in the USA, and 16% of these arrests resulted in the UK officers sustaining an injury.

That's 16% of 6% so basically in about 1% of police arrests UK police officers are injured.

Armed Response:

So far we're looked at cues, personal space and police shootings and what's behind these behaviours. Now let's get a bit more serious.

In the USA, police officers have guns but in the UK our officers don't and personally I'm happy about that.

Therefore, when armed officers are needed which is uncommon in the grand scheme of things. Our UK armed response unit are likely to be drawn in when there's a critical incident that appears to be sufficiently dangerous.

Yet it's getting a mention because not only do these units tend to use lethal force but Barton, Vrij and Bull (2000a, b) argued that this sort of situation might have the potential to encourage suspects to become violent based on the excitation transfer theory of aggression. (Zillmann, 1979, 1982)

It basically proposes that emotional events are physiologically arousing, and people become aware of their physiological arousal due to cues. Such as breathing and sweating.

Then if people fail to recognise the true cause of the emotional arousal then this will result in other factors being identified as the cause of the emotion.

In addition, the internal state the person is experiencing is generally labelled by the person according to the environmental stimuli available at the time.

Practical Terms:

In practical terms what this theory is saying is because of the rapid travel of the armed response units, this is likely to be physiologically arousing and the armed officers are likely to be preparing themselves for a potentially dangerous offender. Since they know they aren't called out for a harmless offender.

Leading to more arousal.

Then if the officer attributes this arousal to the offender, this could result in the labelling the arousal differently.

Making them believe the offender is more dangerous than they might actually be.

Moreover, according to Doerner and Ho (1994) in general officers are great at marksmanship when they appropriately evaluate the incident as a risk to them or their peers.

This accuracy drops if they don't appropriately evaluate the offender as a risk.

Connecting this to theory, if the armed officer attributes the arousal to the offender then there's an increased risk of lethal force being used and the officer could be more aggressive.

If the officer doesn't attribute the arousal then

the officer is likely to be less aggressive towards the offender.

If you want to hear more about the cognitive labelling and the emotions that can create, please check out Biological Psychology Third Edition. I talk about a great case study there.

For another use of the Excitation Transfer theory, please check out Psychology of Relationships.

The Elephant In the Chapter:

No one could do a lethal force chapter any justice whatsoever, without mentioning the disproportionate amount of black people that are killed by police officers compared to white people.

This is not a political book but I do support the Black Lives Matter movement and if you deny this disproportionate isn't real. Then you really are lying to yourself and you're calling all the research and statistics showing this disparity liars too.

However, the disparity is hard to study because it requires very complex methodologies and James, Klinger and Vila (2014) argue that previous research is problematic because it lacks ecological validity and reliable settings.

And that's why it's only mentioned in the chapter because the research is limited. But it's still clear there's a disproportionate amount of black people killed by officers.

I've already spoken about police bias in an earlier chapter but there are topics in Forensic Psychology that are useful here too.

So please read, explore and maybe research it if you're interested.

IMPACT OF POLICE WORK ON OFFICERS

To wrap up the content part of the book, after looking at all of the amazing and exciting topics of interviews, lethal force and police discrimination. We have to look at maybe the most human topics of the book.

And I say this because my background is mainly in clinical psychology and my love for forensic psychology is a side thing.

Therefore, as a person who loves clinical psychology, I really want to look at the officers. To say a cliche I want to look at the brave men and women who protect and serve our communities and in the West, I almost feel the need to remind everyone that we're so lucky that 99% of the time the police are on our side compared to other countries.

So now we need to look at the toll police work has on officers because in this book we have looked at them critically and rightfully criticised their methods, but these officers are still helpful at the end of the day.

As a result whilst police work has a number of negative side effects on the officers themselves, and whilst the data and procedures differs between police forces, there are some forces we can look at.

For example, there's one British police force that requires officers to have an independent counselling session twice a year.

This is excellent because it makes sure people address any concerns they have without the risk of the counsellor telling their boss and the force, unless it meets the criteria for breaking confidentiality. Allowing the officer to get professional help if needed.

In addition, it's important to cast our minds back to the beginning of the book and apply police culture to this. Since the dominant male culture of the police force probably (like it does in mainstream society) discourage male officers from showing signs of so-called weakness and emotion.

Consequently, this counselling session is a great way to overcome and reduce the officer's fear about the dominant police culture learning about their so-called weaknesses and ostracising them because of it.

Furthermore, there has been a lot of recognition around stress having adverse effects on work with Karlsson and Christianson (1990) finding that the following were the most common stressors in police work:

- Being threatened with a weapon
- Taking children into custody
- Notifying next of kin
- Traffic accident. Especially when the officer (tend to be first responders) just arrive to see death and bad injuries.

Leading to a problem of unfortunate outcomes. For instance, 22% of officers felt depressed and 15% felt guilty as well as sleeping problems, nightmares, overreacting and tension were problems too.

Clearly showing the negative outcomes associated with stressful police work.

Nonetheless, it doesn't have to be this way because, just like in clinical psychology, there are coping strategies that can help officers. These are called positive coping strategies, like faith and problem solving, as well as these are associated with less stress.

We all have these positive strategies that help us cope with everyday life. (And no, clinical psychology people, I'm not going to talk about even if these are maladaptive. I have other books for that topic)

For example, I have learning, writing, cooking, exercise and more. So that's another way to think about coping strategies.

Then on the flip side, you have negative and avoidant strategies that were associated with more stress. (Cershon, Narocas, Canton, Ci and Vlaho, 2009)

Interestingly, Rallings (2002) found police officers are hidden suffering victims due to the media and people seem to think officers are immune to what they see and experience.

Such as the general public seems to believe seeing dead bodies, suicidal victims and working on child abduction cases don't affect officers.

Leading to Rallings to make two recommendations:

Firstly, it's possible to focus on only the affected officers and not everyone. Which is great for police forces because it's more cost effective.

Secondly, by examining the immediate effect, it's possible to detect at-risk people immediately and not have to let them suffer before they receive professional help.

Moreover, workplace characteristics can have an impact on whether or not an officer will become psychologically traumatised. Therefore, workplaces should be deemed as supportive, good morale and workplace communications should be improved.

However, if you've listened to my podcast or read any of my other books, you know I'm extremely progressive when it comes to mental health and I agree with the more forward thinking clinical psychologists. But…

I highly doubt this mental health focus on police officers would ever happen within the police work itself because there is still the dominant male culture inside the police force and in the highest levels of our society. As well as in one version of these dominant cultures say mental health is hypered up rubbish and men do NOT show weakness. Period.

And this is the greatest shame of this reality that I highly doubt the police culture would ever focus on the mental health of their officers unless they were made to.

In all honesty, I would love an officer to read this book and prove me wrong. As a clinical psychology person nothing would make me happier.

I just doubt it would happen.

Overall, I want to wrap this book by saying we need to support our police officers, we need to make sure there are the services available to them and the infrastructure in place so if they need help. They can get it.

I don't want any more police officers (or people for that matter) to suffer in silence about their mental health. So I just want everyone to think about that and if there's a police officer reading this for some reason. Then maybe you (or anyone) can make a difference.

Just a thought.

BIBLIOGRAPHY

Barton, J., Vrij, A., & Bull, R. (2000). High speed driving: police use of lethal force during simulated incidents. *Legal and Criminological Psychology*, 5(1), 107-121. https://doi.org/10.1348/135532500168010

Brown, J., Shell, Y. & Cole, T. (2015). Forensic Psychology: Theory, research, policy and practice. 1st edition

Doerner, W.G. (1988), The Impact Of Medical Resources On Criminally Induced Lethality: A Further Examination. Criminology, 26: 171-180. Https://Doi.Org/10.1111/J.1745-9125.1988.Tb00837.X

Howitt, D. (2018). Introduction to forensic and criminal psychology. Essex, UK: Pearson.

6th edition.

Karlsson, Ingemar & Christianson, Sven. (2003). The phenomenology of traumatic experiences in police work. Policing: An International Journal of Police Strategies & Management. 26. 419-438. 10.1108/13639510310489476.

Payne, B. K., Lambert, A. J., & Jacoby, L. L. (2002). Best laid plans: effects of goals on accessibility bias and cognitive control in race-based misperceptions of weapons. *Journal of Experimental Social Psychology, 38*, 384–396.

Plant, E. A., Peruche, B. M., & Butz, D. A. (2005). Eliminating automatic racial bias: making race non-diagnostic for responses to criminal suspects. *Journal of Experimental and Social Psychology, 41*, 141–156.

Whiteley, C (2021) Social psychology: A Guide To Social and Cultural Psychology, Third Edition CGD Publishing.

Whiteley, C (2021) Psychology of Relationships: The Social Psychology of Friendships, Romantic Relationships, Prosocial Behaviour and More, Third Edition

CGD Publishing.

Whiteley, C (2020) Forensic Psychology CGD Publishing.

Whiteley, C (2021) Criminal Profiling, CGD Publishing.

GET YOUR EXCLUSIVE FREE 8 BOOK PSYCHOLOGY BOXSET AND YOUR EMAIL PSYCHOLOGY COURSE HERE!

https://www.subscribepage.com/psychologyboxset

Thank you for reading.

I hoped you enjoyed it.

If you want a FREE book and keep up to date about new books and project. Then please sign up for my newsletter at www.connorwhiteley.net/

Have a great day.

CHECK OUT THE PSYCHOLOGY WORLD PODCAST FOR MORE PSYCHOLOGY INFORMATION!

AVAILABLE ON ALL MAJOR PODCAST APPS.

About the author:

Connor Whiteley is the author of over 30 books in the sci-fi fantasy, nonfiction psychology and books for writer's genre and he is a Human Branding Speaker and Consultant.

He is a passionate warhammer 40,000 reader, psychology student and author.

Who narrates his own audiobooks and he hosts The Psychology World Podcast.

All whilst studying Psychology at the University of Kent, England.

Also, he was a former Explorer Scout where he gave a speech to the Maltese President in August 2018 and he attended Prince Charles' 70th Birthday Party at Buckingham Palace in May 2018.

Plus, he is a self-confessed coffee lover!

POLICE PSYCHOLOGY

All books in 'An Introductory Series':

BIOLOGICAL PSYCHOLOGY 3RD EDITION

COGNITIVE PSYCHOLOGY THIRD EDITION

SOCIAL PSYCHOLOGY- 3RD EDITION

ABNORMAL PSYCHOLOGY 3RD EDITION

PSYCHOLOGY OF RELATIONSHIPS- 3RD EDITION

DEVELOPMENTAL PSYCHOLOGY 3RD EDITION

HEALTH PSYCHOLOGY

RESEARCH IN PSYCHOLOGY

A GUIDE TO MENTAL HEALTH AND TREATMENT AROUND THE WORLD- A GLOBAL LOOK AT DEPRESSION

FORENSIC PSYCHOLOGY

THE FORENSIC PSYCHOLOGY OF THEFT, BURGLARY AND OTHER

RIMES AGAINST PROPERTY

CRIMINAL PROFILING: A FORENSIC PSYCHOLOGY GUIDE TO FBI PROFILING AND GEOGRAPHICAL AND STATISTICAL PROFILING.

CLINICAL PSYCHOLOGY

FORMULATION IN PSYCHOTHERAPY

PERSONALITY PSYCHOLOGY AND INDIVIDUAL DIFFERENCES

CLINICAL PSYCHOLOGY REFLECTIONS VOLUME 1

CLINICAL PSYCHOLOGY REFLECTIONS VOLUME 2

CULT PSYCHOLOGY

Police Psychology

OTHER SHORT STORIES BY CONNOR WHITELEY

Blade of The Emperor

Arbiter's Truth

The Bloodied Rose

Asmodia's Wrath

Heart of A Killer

Emissary of Blood

Computation of Battle

Old One's Wrath

Puppets and Masters

Ship of Plague

Interrogation

Sacrifice of the Soul

Heart of The Flesheater

Heart of The Regent

Heart of The Standing

Feline of The Lost

Heart of The Story

The Family Mailing Affair

Defining Criminality

The Martian Affair

A Cheating Affair

The Little Café Affair

Other books by Connor Whiteley:

The Fireheart Fantasy Series

Heart of Fire

Heart of Lies

Heart of Prophecy

Heart of Bones

Heart of Fate

The Garro Series- Fantasy/Sci-fi

GARRO: GALAXY'S END

GARRO: RISE OF THE ORDER

GARRO: END TIMES

GARRO: SHORT STORIES

GARRO: COLLECTION

GARRO: HERESY

GARRO: FAITHLESS

GARRO: DESTROYER OF WORLDS

GARRO: COLLECTIONS BOOK 4-6

GARRO: MISTRESS OF BLOOD

GARRO: BEACON OF HOPE

GARRO: END OF DAYS

Winter Series- Fantasy Trilogy Books

WINTER'S COMING

WINTER'S HUNT

WINTER'S REVENGE

WINTER'S DISSENSION

Miscellaneous:

THE ANGEL OF RETURN

THE ANGEL OF FREEDOM

POLICE PSYCHOLOGY

Companion guides:

BIOLOGICAL PSYCHOLOGY 2ND EDITION WORKBOOK

COGNITIVE PSYCHOLOGY 2ND EDITION WORKBOOK

SOCIOCULTURAL PSYCHOLOGY 2ND EDITION WORKBOOK

ABNORMAL PSYCHOLOGY 2ND EDITION WORKBOOK

PSYCHOLOGY OF HUMAN RELATIONSHIPS 2ND EDITION WORKBOOK

HEALTH PSYCHOLOGY WORKBOOK

FORENSIC PSYCHOLOGY WORKBOOK

Audiobooks by Connor Whiteley:

BIOLOGICAL PSYCHOLOGY

COGNITIVE PSYCHOLOGY

SOCIOCULTURAL PSYCHOLOGY

ABNORMAL PSYCHOLOGY

PSYCHOLOGY OF HUMAN RELATIONSHIPS

HEALTH PSYCHOLOGY

DEVELOPMENTAL PSYCHOLOGY

RESEARCH IN PSYCHOLOGY

FORENSIC PSYCHOLOGY

GARRO: GALAXY'S END

GARRO: RISE OF THE ORDER

GARRO: SHORT STORIES

GARRO: END TIMES

GARRO: COLLECTION

GARRO: HERESY

GARRO: FAITHLESS

GARRO: DESTROYER OF WORLDS

GARRO: COLLECTION BOOKS 4-6

GARRO: COLLECTION BOOKS 1-6

Business books:

TIME MANAGEMENT: A GUIDE FOR STUDENTS AND WORKERS

LEADERSHIP: WHAT MAKES A GOOD LEADER? A GUIDE FOR STUDENTS AND WORKERS.

BUSINESS SKILLS: HOW TO SURVIVE THE BUSINESS WORLD? A GUIDE FOR STUDENTS, EMPLOYEES AND EMPLOYERS.

BUSINESS COLLECTION

GET YOUR FREE BOOK AT:
WWW.CONNORWHITELEY.NET

www.ingramcontent.com/pod-product-compliance
Lightning Source LLC
LaVergne TN
LVHW011834060526
838200LV00053B/4017